W9-CGR-918

"Vive la France"

"Vive la France"

the french resistance during world war II

by Robert Green

A First Book
Franklin Watts
New York / Chicago / London / Toronto / Sydney

For D. R. Green

Frontis: Two French partisans, wearing looks of grim determination, prepare to engage the Germans in August 1944. Although the Germans occupied all of France by 1944, Resistance members kept the spirit of "Free France" alive.

Cover art by Jane Sterrett

Photographs copyright ©: National Archives, Washington, D.C., United States Memorial Holocaust Museum, photo by Julia Pirotte: p. 2; National Archives: pp.10 (U.S. Signal Corps), 23 (Enemy Records), 29, 56 (both U.S. Information Agency); Wide World Photos: pp. 12, 14, 19, 26, 33; UPI/Bettmann: pp. 15, 17, 25, 31, 35, 37, 39, 51; Archive Photos: pp. 18 (Potter Collection), 42, 44, 46, 49 (Hackett); The Bettmann Archive: p. 21; U.S. Coast Guard Photo: p. 53; British Official Photo: p. 54.

Library of Congress Cataloging-in-Publication Data

Green, Robert, 1969–
    Vive la France : The French Resistance during World War II / by Robert Green.
        p. cm.— (A First book)
        Includes bibliographical references and index.
        ISBN 0-531-20192-9
        1. World War, 1939–1945—Underground movements—France—Juvenile literature. [1. World War, 1939–1945—Underground Movements—France.]
    I. Title. II. Series.
D802.F8G745 1995
940.53'44—dc20   94-22485
                                                                      CIP
                                                                       AC

CONTENTS

INVASION

In 1939, France teetered on the brink of war with Germany. It wouldn't be the first time these two countries had gone to war. Just twenty-one years earlier in World War I, France had helped to defeat Germany. Yet during the years between the two world wars, from 1918 to 1939, Germany recovered faster than France. Most of the battles of World War I had been fought on French territory. The battles had left France in ruins. After the war, a lack of political unity, a poor economy, and other factors kept France from recovering quickly.

Between the two world wars, new beliefs about how a country should be governed sprang up around the world. Communism took root in Russia. Socialism, a political philosophy claiming that wealth should be shared, became popular all over Europe. Fascism sprang up in

Benito Mussolini, the son of a blacksmith and a schoolmistress, rose to become head of Italy's Fascist Party. Mussolini led Italy toward war by forging an alliance with Germany under Adolf Hitler. In a speech, Mussolini dubbed the alliance the Rome–Berlin Axis.

Italy under Benito Mussolini and in Germany under Adolf Hitler. This new political philosophy emphasized all-powerful dictators. It claimed that the strength of a nation was more important than the rights of individuals.

Communism, fascism, and socialism found supporters in France during the years between the wars. Confidence in the democracy of the French Republic weakened as more and more French citizens supported new political parties. Yet French politicians pretended that the French Republic was still strong and unified.

French generals also tried to create a strong image for the country. Knowing that France could never again survive the losses suffered in World War I, they helped build a substantial fortification, known as the Maginot Line, stretching from the border of Belgium to the border of Switzerland. The French generals boasted that this line could never be crossed—that France could not be invaded from the East. The French politicians and generals were very successful in building confidence among their people. But in 1939 France was really like a house of cards—an empty structure held together only by a false sense of security.

By 1918, Germany, too, had become politically unstable and financially bankrupt. In 1919 the Treaty of Versailles outlined the defeated country's bleak future. Germany was forced to accept all responsibility for the war. It was supposed to pay vast sums for wartime damage to all its enemies, especially France. This was bitter news for a country that had just suffered the humiliation of surrender.

The voice of Adolf Hitler emerged from the political

President Woodrow Wilson, seated in the center of this photo taken at the Paris Peace Conference in 1918, attempted to convince England and France to ease their demands on Germany after World War I.

and economic confusion of the 1930s. Hitler's National Socialist Party, or Nazi Party, instilled a bitter pride in the downtrodden Germans. Its call for extreme solutions appealed to their feelings of desperation. Hitler harnessed Germany's bitterness and humiliation to build a fascist regime that ruled by force. He became dictator of the country. As a solution to a German sense of inferiority about losing the war, Hitler claimed that the German people were the master race. He said they were superior to blacks, Gypsies, Slavs, Jews, and many other races and nationalities. About the French, Hitler simply said, "The French are the monkeys of Europe."

Hitler did more than instill a dark sense of pride in the German people. He also put many unemployed Germans back to work. He did this partly by ignoring the restrictions placed on Germany's military in the Treaty of Versailles. Hitler reopened factories and began to produce the weapons of war. He also began to develop an aggressive foreign policy. In 1936, he made an alliance with the Fascist dictator of Italy, Benito Mussolini. Three years later, in 1939, Germany invaded Austria and Czechoslovakia and moved troops into the Rhineland. (The Rhineland is the area to the west of the Rhine River that borders France.) It soon became clear that Hitler and Mussolini were going to gamble for political supremacy over all of Europe.

As Germany sent more and more troops to the border with France, France turned to England for support. Britain's prime minister Neville Chamberlain had been following a policy of appeasement toward the Germans. In other words, Britain had given in to many of Germany's aggressive actions. Chamberlain ignored Germany's new buildup of military power in exchange for promises that Germany would not attack its closest neighbors. This policy provided Hitler with the time needed to build up and position his military. England's policy of appeasement was finally abandoned in 1939 when Germany invaded Poland. France and England honored their alliances with Poland and declared war on Germany. For the second time in the twentieth century Europe found itself in a war.

Rapid industrialization in the 1930s allowed Germany to remilitarize at an alarming rate. Throughout the war German factories continued to produce weapons despite constant bombardment by Allied planes. The machines above, located in an underground factory, produced airplane parts.

French troops scrambled to reinforce the Maginot Line. They were soon joined by a group of British soldiers already in France, known as the British Expeditionary Force. France and Britain waited for battle through a six-month pause known as the "phony war." But during the so-called "phony war," German factories kept forging the weapons of modern warfare. They manufactured tanks, planes, U-Boats (submarines), bombs, and ammunition. Meanwhile France and Germany waited. They even doubted that war was coming their way at all. The French still had complete faith in the strength of Maginot Line.

The belief in the unbeatable strength of the Maginot Line showed how outdated the views of France's aging military leaders really were. The most famous of these leaders was Marshall Henri Philippe Pétain. Pétain was considered the greatest French hero of the First World War. Like his fellow generals, he had little faith in modern military machinery and military strategy. The old generals were prepared to fight another defensive war. They truly believed that the Maginot Line was the greatest defense the French military had ever mustered.

A French general named Charles de Gaulle, once a great admirer of Pétain's, held vastly different views. De Gaulle was thirty-four years younger than Pétain. He believed that the outcome of future wars would be determined by the use of the tank and the airplane. Both of these devices could go around or over permanent lines of defense. De Gaulle's theories of mechanized warfare ruffled the feathers of his superiors. His advice was largely ignored.

German armored divisions (above) easily
pierced French and Belgian lines of defense
in the early days of World War II.

In May 1940 the Germans began pushing westward.
De Gaulle's predictions about the weakness of the outdated French military proved true. The Germans staged
a lightning-fast and highly efficient air and ground assault.
It was known as a blitzkrieg, or "lightning war." The
blitzkrieg overran Denmark in a day. By the end of May,
both Holland and Belgium had fallen to the German

A wounded civilian is evacuated from the French port city of Dunkirk along with French and British troops retreating from the German advance in 1940.

advance. The French army was thrown into confusion as German armored divisions, known as "panzer divisions," sped across northern France. France's great line of defense, the Maginot Line, proved useless. The Germans simply went around it. On June 14, 1940, German tanks rolled into the deserted streets of Paris. The house of cards had collapsed.

2 RESISTANCE AND collaboration

The defeat of France at the hands of the Germans happened quickly and crushed the spirits of the French. It marked the beginning of one of the darkest periods in French history. Some French citizens began to wonder if France as an independent nation had vanished forever.

When the occupation began, France was in a state of chaos. More than three million citizens had fled to Paris in front of the advancing Germans. Once the Germans were in control of Paris, they ordered the French to return to their homes. Luggage, furniture, and every type of belonging left by the fleeing Parisians lined the streets of Paris. The shops were shuttered, and the restaurants were closed. German soldiers had been ordered to aid the French in returning to their homes. Hitler wanted to

In a supreme gesture of contempt for the French people,
German soldiers marched through Paris's Arc de Triomphe
on August 10, 1940. The monument was erected to
celebrate French independence and as a tribute to
soldiers who had died in the service of France.

Taking only what belongings they could carry or squeeze into their crowded vehicles, French citizens fled Paris just days, and in some cases hours, before the German army marched into the deserted streets of the French capital.

On June 14, 1940, German tanks rolled into a village near Malmedy, France. Despite boasts by French generals of the invincibility of France, the German army brushed aside the French army in a matter of a few weeks.

avoid tying up his soldiers in Paris. They could be used at the battle fronts.

The contrast between the Germans and the French just after the fall of Paris was dramatic. The Germans appeared strong, calm, confident and, to some degree, cheerful. Their soldiers formed orderly columns and had neatly tailored uniforms. The French, on the other hand, returned to Paris uncertain and afraid. They came in large confused mobs, carrying clothes, food, and infants. The French became second-class citizens in their own country. Many of their rights were suspended.

In 1941, some French citizens defied the rules of German occupation and celebrated the French national holiday of Bastille Day. The Nazis shot one celebrant for singing the outlawed national anthem and another for insulting the German military. It was becoming clear that resistance to German occupation would cost the French dearly.

To force the French to cooperate, the Germans kept holding more than one million French prisoners. Nevertheless, French resistance to German occupation arose. It arose spontaneously and in many different forms. In its mildest form it was simply peaceful noncooperation. A French citizen would give wrong directions to German soldiers or pretend not to understand when a German soldier asked for help or information.

Graffiti became increasingly common in Paris. In the dark of night, anti-German slogans or patriotic sayings, such as *"Vive la France"* ("Long Live France"), were scrawled in public places. There is a French province

The Cross of Lorraine, flying on this flag, became a symbol of resistance to Nazi and Vichy authority, as well as the official emblem of the Free French Forces under General Charles de Gaulle.

called Lorraine that borders Germany. Throughout history, Germany has often tried to claim Lorraine as its own. The Cross of Lorraine, which was the symbol of the province, now became the symbol of French independence and resistance. In fact, the Cross of Lorraine was the most popular graffiti image in occupied Paris. These meager beginnings were the acts of a few proud and indignant citizens. But from these and other small acts the Resistance would become a dangerous threat to the Nazi occupation.

The first organized Resistance groups banded together to smuggle out of France those French and British officers and soldiers who were in hiding. Safe routes to England and Sweden by sea were forged. Other routes led to Spain and Switzerland by land. Later in the war, as part of the German plan for racial purification, Jews in danger of being sent to Germany for extermination as well as Frenchmen in danger of being forced into the German army escaped along the same underground routes.

Some French soldiers in hiding decided to organize armed Resistance groups to actively fight the Germans.

The ranks of these groups grew slowly. Each member would recruit a few trustworthy acquaintances. They had to operate in the strictest secrecy so as not to be discovered by the Germans. What is more, they were very poorly armed. While these seeds of resistance were being planted in Occupied France, the Germans were helping to carve a new French State out of the southeastern corner of France.

The Germans had divided France into two sections. The North of France along with the Atlantic coastal strip in western France was called the "Occupied Zone" and was ruled directly by the Nazi government. In the southeastern corner of France, Hitler allowed Marshall Pétain to create a semi-independent state. It was Pétain who had formally surrendered France to Germany and its ally Italy on June 10, 1940. Pétain's new semi-independent French state was known as Vichy France because its capital was the small resort town of Vichy. It was also known simply as Unoccupied France.

Pétain believed that France had lost the war because of its moral weakness. He charged that the politicians of the old French Republic were immoral and irresponsible. He abolished the parliamentary system and gave himself almost unlimited powers to govern. Seeing an opportunity to gain power, French fascists flocked to Vichy France. Indeed, Pétain's government had many of the signs of fascism. It was dictatorial and morally judgmental. It emphasized the rights of the state over the rights of the individual.

Pétain portrayed himself as the savior of France. He

Henri Philippe Pétain (left), an aging hero of World War I, formally surrendered France to Germany in June 1940. Hitler (right) allowed Pétain to establish a French government in an enclave of unoccupied French territory to avoid using German troops for occupation when they could be used elsewhere for combat.

claimed that only under his leadership could France survive. He said that the defeat of France was caused by the lack of virtue in the nation. This was supposedly the result of lazy, greedy politicians and an immoral population. While Pétain called for a return to the values of work, family, and country, his chief minister, Pierre Laval, collaborated with the German conqueror. Laval and other prominent Vichy supporters, such as French admiral and politician Jean François Louis Darlan, hoped that France would play an important role in Hitler's dream of a "Greater Germany." By a "Greater Germany," Hitler meant a solid economic block stretching from Eastern Europe to the Atlantic Ocean and controlled by Germany.

On October 24, 1940, Pétain met with Hitler for the first time. A single handshake between Pétain and Hitler caused many French citizens to shake their heads in sorrow and mourn the loss of France. The Marshall spoke openly of whole-hearted cooperation with the Germans to build the "new European order." Some Vichy supporters believed that France, which had been settled by Germanic tribes such as the Franks, could make the new Germanic invasion part of French identity. German and French fascists were counting on the fact that many French had always distrusted the English. For some, the failure of the English to aid the French when the Germans invaded had increased anti-English feeling. Fascist propaganda was designed to drive French sympathies away from Britain and closer to Hitler's Germany.

Meanwhile, Resistance groups in Vichy France grew. They started to target Pétain's government as well as the Germans. On June 22, 1941, Germany attacked the

These members of a French underground fighting unit raise the French tricolor on a makeshift flagpole. The offense was punishable by death.

Soviet Union. This had a dramatic effect on the Resistance movement in Occupied and Vichy France. Communists in France were already against the policies of Vichy France and the fascist government of Hitler. Now

The government of Unoccupied France, pictured above, gave many unimportant beauraucrats the opportunity to seize power. The two figures in the center are Henri Philippe Pétain (right) and Pierre Laval. After the war, military courts found both men guilty of war crimes.

they had a reason to become even more active in their fight against Vichy France and the occupying Germans. The Communists in France looked to the Communist government of Joseph Stalin in the Soviet Union for support.

War with the Soviet Union also increased the collaboration between the French Fascist Party, led by Jacques Doriot, and Nazi Germany. Doriot's Fascist Party and other ultra-conservative groups formed the Légion des Volontaires Français contre le Bolchevisme (Legion of French Volunteers Against Bolshevism, or the LVF). The Legion vowed to fight for Hitler on the eastern front against the communist Russians. The Fascists believed that all communists were their enemies. Doriot himself marched east with the first group of volunteers. LVF soldiers vowed obedience directly to Hitler and had the respect and blessings of Pétain. Those already in disagreement with the policies of Pétain were scandalized by the lengths to which French fascists would go to please Hitler.

In 1943, the Vichy government police added shock troops to its ranks. This group, called the Milice, struck more fear and loathing into the French than the Germans. It was fanatically anti-Jewish, anti-Resistance, and pro-Nazi. Other special police units were established in Vichy France to handle Jewish "questions." These units helped deport Jews to concentration camps in Germany.

In Germany during this time Jews were required to wear a yellow, six-pointed star, known as the Star of David, so that they could be identified by all. Even though this was not the case in France, French Jews were still banned from most types of jobs. They suffered prejudice, physical attacks, and sometimes deportation or execution. Under the guise of moral savior, the Vichy government was becoming nothing more than a puppet government controlled by Hitler.

3 DE GAULLE AND THE "FREE FRENCH"

In the final days before the fall of France, some unyielding French citizens had refused to accept the German occupation. They had fled to England or the French colonies in North Africa to carry on the fight. Among those who had fled was General Charles de Gaulle.

De Gaulle boarded a plane for England just before the Nazis marched into Paris. From there he independently launched a campaign to keep French forces in the war. He met with other French soldiers and sailors who were in England and sought the support of the English and American governments.

De Gaulle's first act was to condemn the Vichy government. He publicly denounced Pétain as a defeatist, a puppet of the Germans, and a traitor to France. Pétain returned the sentiments. Although de Gaulle was in

England, Vichy officials tried him for treason and desertion, found him guilty, and sentenced him to death. Both Pétain and later de Gaulle claimed to head the legitimate government of France. Pétain continued to rely on the help of the Nazis. De Gaulle ran his exiled French government from England.

Many exiled governments had taken refuge in England when the Germans invaded their countries. These included the Belgians, the Dutch, and the Norwegians. But none was as arrogant, as demanding, and as attention-getting as the self-proclaimed French government in exile of General Charles de Gaulle. At the time, few British and American officials knew who he was. Most found him difficult to deal with. He had prickly relations with both the new British prime minister Winston Churchill and U.S. president Franklin Delano Roosevelt. Even many of de Gaulle's fellow French—especially military officers—were shocked when he began to speak in the name of the French government.

Then why did anyone listen to this tall, lanky, stubborn patriot? For the most part, his declaration of a government in exile was a trick. De Gaulle was well aware that the Allied powers were looking for someone to represent the French outside of Vichy. De Gaulle's big advantage was his attractive public personality. Even if the allied governments hesitated to recognize him as the exiled leader of France, his silver-tongued charm would win the sympathy of those who heard his remarkable speeches.

The British Broadcast Corporation (BBC) granted de Gaulle air time on the radio. His broadcasts echoed

British prime minister Winston Churchill (seated right) and U.S. president Franklin Roosevelt (seated left) meet with Gen. Charles de Gaulle (standing right) and High Commissioner of French Africa Gen. Henri Giraud in Casablanca, Morocco, in 1943.

throughout the Western world, including France and America. While Pétain called for total cooperation with the Germans, de Gaulle called for active resistance, sacrifice, and, most of all, hope. In his first address, he invited all French citizens to join him in resisting Nazi occupation.

At first, few heard his call. In France, however, more and more people tuned in to the BBC to hear news that was not controlled by the Germans. After hearing the BBC news programs, the occupied French heard de Gaulle's stirring speeches. The Germans soon outlawed BBC broadcasts, but, secretly, people continued to listen.

De Gaulle called his government in exile the "Free French" government. Slowly, daring French men and women escaped from France to join de Gaulle. They came in boats and in planes, and always at great risk.

De Gaulle formed an organization for spying and collection of military information. It was known as the Central Bureau of Information and Action (BCRA). Its main purpose was to supply the Allies with military information coming out of occupied France. The BCRA also sent agents to occupied France by plane, boat, and submarine. These agents were responsible for training resistance members, sabotaging military targets, and rescuing important civilians from the Nazis.

In an attempt to unify Resistance efforts in France, de Gaulle sent an envoy, Jean Moulin, to France on January 1, 1942. At the time of the German invasion, Moulin had been a local government official in the town of Chartres. When the Germans captured Chartres, they had demanded that Moulin sign a document claiming that

French soldiers, called poilus, seize a moment of rest to write letters to their families in France, at a railway station in England. The British Royal Navy carried these soldiers to safety after the fall of France.

French soldiers were responsible for the destruction caused by Germans during the invasion. Moulin had cut his own throat rather than yield to the German demand. But surprisingly, he survived. After recuperating, he had escaped to England where he had joined de Gaulle.

Sending Moulin back to France to head the Resistance proved to be a tricky job indeed. Each Resistance organization was headed by a leader who greedily protected his power. The secrecy and loose organization of the groups prevented most of their leaders from knowing even the number of members or supplies in each group. The many different Resistance groups also had many different political aims. For example, the Communists regarded de Gaulle as an enemy. At no point during the occupation was de Gaulle's dream of a united Resistance movement fulfilled. Nevertheless, de Gaulle became a symbol of the entire Resistance to the rest of the world.

De Gaulle's envoy Moulin became the highest-ranking "Free French" official in France. He also became a link among the many Resistance groups and de Gaulle. Moulin would prove to be one of the most famous of all Resistance fighters. He worked tirelessly to throw off the yoke of Nazi occupation.

The second most important figure in the Resistance was Moulin. His hoarse voice and ever-present scarf—used to hide the scars of his suicide attempt—became famous among the French. They admired his courage to return to France after his terrifying encounter with the Nazis. His efforts to unite the Resistance groups failed, but he provided many of them with a link to England and the supplies that the English could provide.

During a meeting of Resistance leaders, a Frenchman leaked Moulin's whereabouts to German intelligence. The Gestapo, which was the German secret police, captured

General de Gaulle chats with French pilots at an airstrip in England. Not only French fliers, but also pilots from other occupied countries (such as Poland, Belgium, and Czechoslovakia) who had escaped to England (some with their aircraft) joined Allied assaults in the air.

Moulin and the others. Moulin died in the hands of Gestapo interrogators on July 8, 1943. De Gaulle, however, continued the fight with increasing help from the Allied powers.

4 aid from the allies

At first, the United States was not prepared to fight another world war. The U.S. attempted to remain neutral during the early days of the war in Europe. Then Japan bombed the American Pacific fleet in Pearl Harbor, Hawaii, on December 7, 1941. America immediately declared war on Japan. Germany and Italy declared war on the United States three days later. U.S. entry into the war tipped the scales in favor of an Allied victory. The United States had vast resources for equipment and enough people for a large army.

Even inside occupied France, the influence of the United States could be felt. By 1942, Resistance groups were being supplied by three separate sources: Britain, de Gaulle, and the United States. As the ranks of the Resistance swelled the need for supplies grew. Air drops from any source were desperately needed.

As the war dragged on, the Germans experimented with rockets that were fired from the ground and which plunged down upon England with deadly consequences. The wreckage in this picture resulted from a German rocket attack on a London marketplace.

The Allied powers were slowly realizing the usefulness of Resistance information flowing out of France. The British were especially grateful when Resistance agents discovered two German secret weapons—the V1 "buzz bombs" and the V2 sonic rockets. These unmanned rockets were fired from ramps resembling ski jumps. They could easily reach Britain from launch sites in German-occupied territory. Anti-aircraft weapons could not stop the rockets. The Allies needed exact information about launch sites so they could destroy the rockets while they were still on the ground.

One particularly successful Resistance agent, Wladyslaw Wazny, discovered more than one hundred V1 launch sites before he was shot by German patrols.

Allied powers began forging their own links to Resistance groups and dispatched their own agents to occupied and Vichy France. The helped the Resistance smuggle important strategic information out of the country.

By the time the United States became involved with the French Resistance, the British were already sending aid to Resistance groups. In early 1941, the British had organized Special Operations Executive, Section France (SOE/F). Its purpose was the direct supply of Resistance groups in France. The SOE/F had begun without de Gaulle's knowledge. For a long time it competed with de Gaulle's own Resistance movement, the BCRA. Finally, the British formed Special Operations Executive, Section Resistance/France (SOE R/F). This operation was designed to directly support de Gaulle's BCRA.

Men and women who had been recruited for SOE/F were highly trained in the arts of secret warfare at such places as Beaulieu Manor, in Southampton, England, and the Government Code and Cipher School at Bletchely Park. In these stately manor houses agents learned how to jump from planes, use explosives, code and decode messages, and operate radios. All agents were supplied

Battle-weary German soldiers in North Africa rest after their desert offensive against the British position at El Alamein, Egypt, failed in 1942. The successful defense of El Alamein proved to be a turning point in the war. The four corners of this photograph are adorned with the swastika, a symbol of Nazi Germany.

with a lethal L-Pill. If they were captured they could escape torture and execution by suicide.

After training, SOE agents landed by air or sea behind enemy lines. Here they would have the chance to put into action their newly learned skills. In 1942, the Americans formed their own version of SOE called the Office of Strategic Services (OSS). This organization was the foundation for today's Central Intelligence Agency. OSS personnel and operations merged with SOE in 1943. American and British agents parachuted into occupied France to gather intelligence and train Resistance groups.

By 1944, more than five hundred OSS agents were operating in France. OSS agents were also in close contact with supporters of de Gaulle in the French colonies in North Africa. Here they gained intelligence about the German Afrika Corps—Hitler's troops in Africa. They also helped refugees fleeing occupied France through Spain into French North Africa.

English and American forces launched a large-scale invasion of French North Africa, called Operation Torch. They swarmed through Morocco, Algeria, and Tunisia. The success of Operation Torch greatly altered the course of the war. It provided the Allies with strategic ports from which to attack Hitler's stranglehold on Europe. Realizing the threat, Germany swiftly invaded Vichy France to protect the German Army's southern flank. France, like many other European countries, was now entirely and directly under Nazi control.

THE
SECRET
WAR

Because the Germans occupied all of France, Resistance groups had many chances for direct contact with their enemies. They began to take advantage of the situation. They cut communication lines. They derailed supply trains. They blew up ammunition dumps and assassinated German officers. Underground newspapers and radio broadcasts operated secretly throughout the occupation. They reported successful Resistance operations and kept the people informed of Allied victories.

Special German "radio play" units patrolled in search of these secret broadcasters. The German squads were camouflaged as repair trucks or other common vehicles. The disguised units crept along the path directed by their homing devices and seized radio operators working for

the Resistance. Resistance broadcasters who were caught by the Germans were tortured into revealing their codes. Then the Germans used the codes to relay false information to the Allies. This caused Allied planes to drop supplies, weapons, and agents directly into the lap of the waiting Germans.

By 1943, the Resistance had as many losses as those of a regular army. More than a thousand members had been killed and forty thousand members had been arrested for engaging in Resistance activities. Entire Resistance organizations had been betrayed by pro-Nazi Frenchmen. Or they had been tracked by German spies or the German Gestapo and French Milice.

The Gestapo conducted periodic sweeps, known as "Rat-hunts." Houses were searched. Flat-bottomed boats patrolled the murky waters of the Paris sewer system. Suspects were rounded up. In Paris, catacombs provided concealment for Resistance members on the run. The catacombs were underground passageways that had been built many hundreds of years ago by the Romans. But even with the catacombs the odds were not in favor of Resistance members.

To avoid being picked up by the Germans, Resistance members traveled through the shadowy waterways and tunnels beneath the city of Paris. The inscription above the entrance to the tunnel pictured here translates, "Stop! This is the empire of the dead."

Resistance members used these ancient catacombs,
lined with the bones of Paris's dead, for clandestine
meetings and to store weapons. German
intelligence agents conducted regular sweeps,
called "rat hunts," of these eerie passageways.

The Germans took ruthless revenge on the Resistance. German authorities often demanded large public fines, often in the millions of francs, as payment for acts of sabotage. Resistance members were dealt long prison sentences or, more commonly, shot. For each German assassinated by the Resistance, the Germans executed ten French hostages (still held from the early days of the war). This figure continued to increase as the war went on.

Despite heavy losses, Resistance numbers continued to grow. Their actions became more and more daring. On the average, Resistance members assassinated more than three German soldiers a day in 1943. De Gaulle pleaded with them to stop the assassinations. He did not think the execution of handfuls of French hostages a worthwhile exchange for one German life. But the Resistance ignored him. After all, as early as 1943, the Germans had ordered all French males older than age twenty to work in German factories or defense installations. For many French, such direct aiding of the German war effort was intolerable.

In the countryside new Resistance groups formed. A Corsican word, *maquis* (ma-KEE), used to describe the foliage that covered the hilly areas of Corsica, became the name for these groups. Members of the maquis, called maquisards, took to the mountainous areas of southern France and the western province of Brittany, where they engaged the Germans in guerilla warfare.

The effectiveness of a particular maquis group depended on how many weapons and explosives they

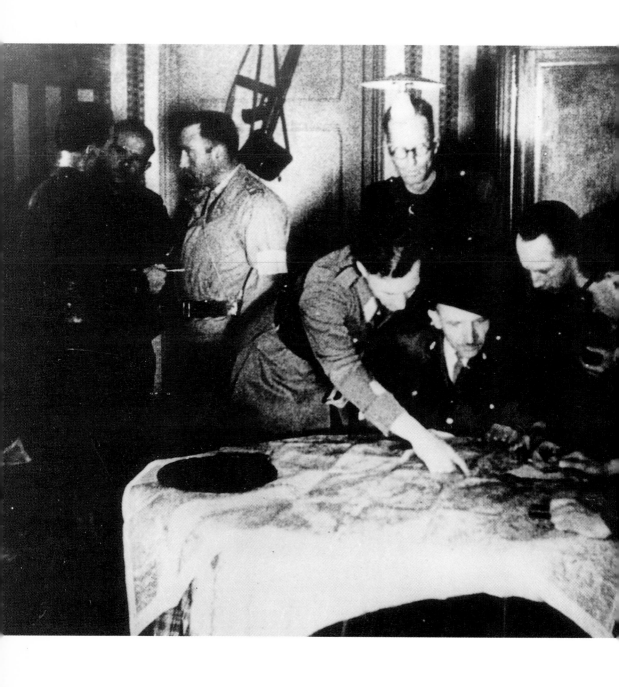

had. Leaders encouraged maquisards to use the few weapons that they had to get more. Their motto was, "Each weapon should bring in at least one other weapon every week." Despite lack of supplies, the maquis carried out successful attacks on German positions, especially German rail lines. Rail workers, telephone operators, and others who were sympathetic to the Resistance provided the maquis with exact timetables of German troop and supply movements.

Before the Allied invasion of France, the maquis had already freed a number of towns and rural areas from German control. Nowhere was success more decisive than on Corsica itself. Corsica is a Mediterranean island that is governed by France. On this island, the maquis were more than ten thousand strong by 1943.

Aided by some Italian troops who had joined their side, the maquis of Corsica attacked the Germans on September 8. The Germans surrendered less than a month later. The maquis had driven some forty-two thousand German troops from Corsica. They had liberated this French territory with little help from the Allies.

A French general and his staff members plan an attack on a German position from within Occupied France. Maquis groups, like the one pictured here, diverted German troops from battlefronts by launching attacks in the French countryside.

6 libERATiON

By the spring of 1944, the war had turned in favor of the Allied powers. The German Army had suffered heavy losses on the Eastern Front fighting against the Russians. Stalin had pleaded with the Allies for the start of a second battlefront as early as 1941. Finally, the Allies prepared for the invasion of France. They code-named the invasion Operation Overlord.

The Allies recognized the value of Resistance support for a large-scale invasion. Resistance leaders claimed to be soldiers already in place for fighting. The Allies began including the Resistance movements into their invasion plans. Resistance groups were assigned three main duties. They were to provide a constant source of spy information about German targets and German counter-invasion maneuvers. They were to destroy German com-

A Resistance member secretly transmits information from a radio hidden in a large wardrobe. The Resistance provided invaluable information to Allied Command in London. The transmitter was probably either homemade or dropped by an Allied plane.

munication and transportation links. And finally they were to distract the Germans with small attacks on their positions.

Resistance agents provided detailed reports on German fortifications on the Atlantic coast of France, which was called the Atlantic wall. When the Allies did invade, they had exact diagrams of the wall, including all of its strong and weak points, its surrounding tank traps, and its mine fields. The Resistance also supplied detailed information about German troop strength and troop location. The reports were stunningly accurate.

The Allies mustered a force of almost three million men and women for the Overlord invasion. On June 6, 1944, known as D-Day, Allied forces landed on the beaches of Normandy, a province in northwestern France.

By this time the ranks of the Resistance had swelled. Though the Allies were dropping more supplies than ever before, volunteers far out-numbered weapons. Allied agents parachuted into occupied France in enormous numbers to give last-minute weapons and explosives training.

When the BBC broadcast a coded signal, the Resistance sprang into action. Rail and phone lines were cut, roads and tunnels were blocked, electrical stations were blown, and bridges were destroyed. German forces scrambled to reinforce the front at Normandy. But Resistance units attacked their troop and supply convoys, slowing German defensive maneuvers.

Resistance action on D-Day was a stunning success. So successful were the joint maneuvers of the Resistance and Allied forces that the entire invasion ran

American paratroopers prepare to jump over Occupied France on June 6, 1944 (D-Day). Resistance groups provided important diagrams of German defensive positions so that paratroopers would know exactly what to expect when they reached the ground. Nevertheless, the Germans flooded the coastal plains of Normandy and littered the ground with booby traps to harass the paratroopers after landing.

ahead of schedule. By August, Resistance action had cleared invasion routes through Provence in southern France. The Allies liberated the city of Grenoble nearly three months sooner than they had expected; Marseilles was freed almost a month early; Lyons, seventy-two days early. The fierce drive forced the Germans to retreat. The first German troops crawled back to Germany.

De Gaulle's officials followed the Allied Armies. They replaced Vichy officials in newly liberated villages, towns, and cities. De Gaulle arrived in his beloved homeland just a week after the D-Day invasion. He toured France and then visited foreign powers on diplomatic missions. He was attempting to secure personal support as the leader of liberated France. After de Gaulle met with U.S. president Franklin D. Roosevelt, the Americans recognized de Gaulle and his administration as the temporary government of France. This was the recognition for which de Gaulle was looking.

Under the command of U.S. general George Patton, Allied armored units neared Paris at the start of August 1944. But the Allied High Command ordered Patton not

The U.S. Navy deposits soldiers, tanks, support vehicles, and supplies on a beach at Normandy. German general Erwin Rommel was responsible for securing the defenses of coastal France against an Allied invasion. Rommel knew that if the Allies got a foothold on French soil, the war would speed to an end.

to take Paris. They predicted that high casualties would be suffered in the fighting needed to liberate a large city. They also felt that the risk of destroying one of the oldest and most beautiful capitals in Europe was too high. The French, however, had other ideas.

On the morning of August 19, the Parisian police marched to the Paris Prefecture, which contained the offices of the city administration. They declared that they were resisting German occupation. Quickly Resistance groups emerged from hiding. Soon thereafter, more citizens rallied to the call to arms. The city was in open revolt. Hitler had ordered that Paris be held. He knew that if he lost Paris he would lose France. If the Germans had to leave Paris, Hitler wanted the city to be left in flames.

The Germans reacted to the street fighting somewhat halfheartedly. Gen. Dietrich von Choltitz, the German officer in command of Paris, was convinced that Hitler was mentally unstable. He thought that Germany would lose the war in the weeks or months to come. He did not want to go down in history as the destroyer of

After nearly five years of German occupation, French citizens cheer on a British tank as it speeds through the historic village of Beauvais. The French received most Allied troops with relief, but some French citizens, angered by the destruction caused by Allied bombs in France, resented the presence of Allied soldiers.

Paris. So he negotiated a temporary cease-fire with Resistance leaders after only one afternoon of fighting. The cease-fire held, but the fighting never really stopped. Parisians built barricades in the streets and skirmishes broke out all over the city. The French armored division on the outskirts of Paris pleaded with the Allied command to join the fight. Finally, after much confusion, Allied tanks rolled into Paris.

The Germans held out until August 25, when the last fanatical Nazi troops were routed out of their positions. General Choltitz surrendered. De Gaulle entered the city, greeted by joyously tearful crowds. De Gaulle was the lone voice from London, who had succeeded in garnering the support of the Allies for the Free French and the Resistance. Now he marched down the Champs Elysées, the central avenue of Paris, flanked by some of the other victorious Resistance leaders, amidst the cheers of liberated French citizens.

Gen. Charles de Gaulle inspects French and American troops who participated in recent combat in Alsace, a French province that borders Germany. De Gaulle was elected provisional president of the French Republic. He latter served as president of France from 1958 to 1969.

Afterword

A great deal of ugliness followed the liberation of France. An outcry of frustration and anger swept through Resistance and non-Resistance members alike. In some instances, collaborators and suspected collaborators were tried, illegally and without representation. These trials came to be known as "popular trials." The suspected collaborators were accused, and, having no chance to defend themselves, promptly shot.

Another example of this type of mob justice concerned French women who had been seen with the German soldiers or who had had children by them. Their heads were shaved in large public gatherings, while the crowd hurled insults at them. There are no accurate records to show how often these public humiliations occurred, but the mood among many French citizens was a mood of vengeance.

In a more official setting, the leaders of Vichy France were tried as war criminals. In 1945, the French High Court of Justice condemned Marshall Philippe Pétain and Pierre Laval to death. Laval was shot. In consideration of Pétain's age—eighty-nine—and his heroic service in World War I, his punishment was reduced to life imprisonment. Pétain lingered in prison until his death in 1951.

De Gaulle was elected provisional president of the French Republic. However, he resigned from the presidency in 1946. Throughout the war de Gaulle had tried to limit the political power of Resistance groups with different political aims, such as the Communists. Once in power, de Gaulle largely refused to recognize the contributions of Communist and Socialist Resistance groups. In fact, much of his political life after the war was spent fighting political groups sympathetic to Communism or Socialism.

It may never be known exactly how many people actively resisted the German occupation in France. After the war, some Resistance groups exaggerated their importance. And, not surprisingly, most French citizens claimed to have been in the Resistance. Writer Jean-Paul Sartre, who had been a member of the Resistance, had this to say: "It should be remembered that active resistance was necessarily limited to a minority. And I think that that minority, by accepting martyrdom deliberately and without hope, has more than redeemed our weakness."

for further reading

Nonfiction

Aaseng, Nathan. *Paris*. New York: New Discovery, 1992.

Schur, Maxine. *Hannah Szenes: A Song of Light*. Philadelphia: Jewish Publication Society of America, 1986.

Shea, George. *The Silent Hero: A True Escape Story from World War II*. New York: Random House, 1994.

Fiction

Dank, Milton. *The Dangerous Game*. New York: Dell, 1981.

Index

about the author

Robert Green is a freelance writer who lives in New York City. He holds a B.A. in English literature from Boston University and is presently writing a series of biographies of important figures of the ancient world.